REACHING IMPOSSIBLE LIMITS

EFFORTLESS TECHNIQUES TO BECOMING A STRONGER, SLIMMER, HEALTHIER, AND FASTER TOP PERFORMER

Benoit Fabreguettes

Print ISBN: 978-1-54397-567-3

eBook ISBN: 978-1-54397-568-0

Disclaimer

The material in this book is for informational purposes only.

Some of the methods and exercises described in this book are not suitable for pregnant women or people with any medical issues, high blood pressure, or depression. We recommend that you learn these techniques with a certified instructor and that you obtain a medical practitioner's advice before practicing the methods outlined in this book. The techniques described are not intended to treat or cure any health problems. The author is not a medical practitioner.

The author and publisher expressly disclaim responsibility for any adverse effects that may result from the practices contained in this book.

Table of Contents

Part F: Pillar 4 - Cold Exposure

Part G: Pillar 5 – Physical Strength

Acknowledgments

To the chain of teachers who kept the techniques described in this book alive through millennia.

To my friends who reviewed my book and provided me their feedback—Alexandre, Andrew, Anthony, Dominic, Graham, Jag, Laurent, Lénaïc, Marie-Eve, and Myrna.

To all of the people who shared their stories during workshops and seminars.

Finally, to my parents, Françoise and Vincent; my brother, his wife, and my niece, Thibault, Eva, and Clarisse, for their love and support through this journey.

Thank you all.

Foreword

Welcome to Reaching Impossible Limits

Effortless Techniques for Becoming a Stronger, Slimmer, Healthier, and Faster Top Performer

---

An overview of this book

│ 326 words │ 2 minutes' reading time │

Foreword

This book is not a story to portray the life of successful artists, athletes, greatest inventors, and business founders. *Reaching Impossible Limits* is a method to reach our own goals though removing the limitations of our abilities and maximizing our body performance. Huge scientific advances in understanding how our bodies work stress the following limitations to becoming a stronger, slimmer, healthier, and faster top performer:

1. Being always connected—no time to relax.

2. Social pressures—you believe your peers have a better life, as evidenced by their social media profiles.

3. Multi-tasking—the brain does not actually have the ability to do two things at the same time.

4. Lifestyle factors—pressure to be always perfect.

I wrote this book to share efficient methods of mind and body control through an accessible framework that will provide day-to-day positive results. Most of these methods have been used for centuries but forgotten as people moved away from traditional philosophies toward more medicine-based cures. Once you understand the simple methods in this book, the only trick is to practice.

The responsibility for becoming a stronger, slimmer, healthier, and faster top performer is in your hands. Success is in your grasp.

Content
- Part A summarizes the best techniques and exercises to build up the most complete existing program—the *Reaching Impossible Limits* method.

- Part B, pillar 1 explores the limitless power of the body through learning how to use the mind in order to achieve unthinkable goals.

- Part C, pillar 2 shows how to achieve strong concentration through the power of meditation and living stress-free.

- Part D highlights the power of breathing—through science, techniques, and extraordinary abilities.

- Part E, pillar 3 stresses scientifically proven techniques to go beyond known limits.

- Part F, pillar 4 provides exercises to quickly and easily re-enforce the immune system through the cold.

- Part H, pillar 5 speeds the learning process of the exercises described in this book through developing a day-to-day healthy lifestyle.

Introduction

Welcome to My Beliefs

Free Your Unbelievable Power Using Proven Techniques

Why I created *Reaching Impossible Limits* through a combination of successful methods

│ 538 words │ 6 minutes' reading time │

Introduction

My beliefs changed one day in July 2015. That particular day I was bored, watching videos on YouTube, when I ran across a VICE documentary about someone who called himself "the Iceman." In the documentary *Inside the Superhuman World of the Iceman*, Wim Hof stated he could train anyone to swim into frozen water and climb mountains under extreme conditions while only wearing shorts.

When I read or watch such extraordinary results, I never say it is impossible; I have always been open-minded and curious about non-traditional methods like the one Hof was describing. I believe there will always be some lag time between reports of inexplicable phenomena and science providing an explanation of the same.

On the other hand, neither do I accept nor reject something as true because my teacher or anyone else tells me it is so; I use the value of self-experimentation to test exercises, to generate efficient programs, and to develop innovative methods. I am proactively skeptical, not defensively skeptical.

That is why I decided to go to Poland to follow a five-day workshop based on the method developed by Wim Hof. I did not know what to expect but figured that, in a worst-case scenario, I could lose a five-day vacation and €1,300.

The training, led by Kasper Van Der Meulen, a certified Wim Hof trainer, changed my perception of life. I was one of a diverse group of twenty-five people—ranging from musicians to consultants, from a healthy person to a sick person, from a sportsman to a sedentary woman. By the end of the workshop, every single one of us had succeeded in climbing two mountains under extreme conditions, with temperatures around -20°C (-4°F), wearing shorts only. No one lost a finger or suffered frostbite.

At that moment, I decided to test all non-traditional wellness methods with a neutral point of view, and I started training daily, setting a new goal every quarter. For each goal, the only thing that mattered was the impact on my wellness and performance.

From a health and wellness point of view, I have never been stronger than I've been since 2015. In addition, these past four years, I have never been sick or used medication. When I feel I am getting sick, I practice intense breathing for fifteen minutes. Then I am back to normal.

Talking freely about non-ordinary methods without judgment with colleagues and friends led to the founding of the *Reaching Impossible Limits* program. Rather than reinventing the wheel, I've combined the best scientifically proven techniques and ancient well-known exercises I've encountered to create a more efficient and results-oriented method. *Reaching Impossible Limits* is a tool to becoming a stronger, slimmer, healthier, and faster top performer.

The *Reaching Impossible Limits* method is accessible to everyone (unless not recommended by your medical practitioner). It's composed of five main pillars described in the following chapters.

Everything explained in the book works; I have personally tested and practiced it all. I believe these combinations of universal techniques will be effective for you as well, with your own unique adjustments as necessary.

You were born to learn; you are a natural-born learner. Be open-minded, try it, learn from your results, and you will *Reach Impossible Limit.*

Part A

The Reaching Impossible Limits Method

Impossible Doesn't Exist

Chapter 1

Strategy to Succeed

These first two chapters provide a summary of the best exercises to create the most efficient program to become a stronger, slimmer, healthier, and faster top performer. These exercises as a whole are called the *Reaching Impossible Limits* method.

The *Reaching Impossible Limits* method is a combination of the ancient/classic strategies I have found to be the most effective on my self-help journey to health and wellness. The method is composed of five main pillars that interact with each other. Each pillar and exercise is explained in detail in the following chapters.

The first three pillars—unbreakable mental fortitude, strong concentration, and a perfect breathing pattern—are the foundation of *Reaching Impossible Limits*. These three pillars are absolutely essential prerequisites in your daily practice. If you only have five minutes, always select one exercise from each of the first three pillars (beginning from the bottom of the following pyramid of pillars).

The Reaching Impossible Limits Pillars

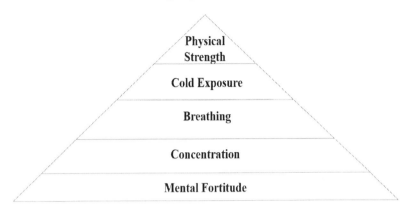

Pillar 1 - Mental Fortitude

Your state of mind is the foundation of success. You must believe in your goals and abilities. Pillar 1 influences your mind to remove the existence of doubts.

Pillar 2 - Concentration

Nothing will stop you if you have unbreakable concentration. Pillar 2 increases your positive attitude, determination, and focus, making it possible to never be discouraged and always move forward toward your goals through the power of meditation.

Pillar 3 - Breathing

Developing and learning a perfect breathing pattern leads to becoming healthier, slimmer, and more productive.

Pillar 4 - Cold Exposure

Cold exposure strengthens your nervous system, immune system, and mental attitude. It leads to being stronger and healthier and increases your willpower.

Pillar 5 - Physical Strength

Physical exercises regenerate your mind, strengthen your body, and produce a sensation of feeling great.

A Four-Week Plan

The *Reaching Impossible Limits* program is a combination that works for me. I do believe that it can and will be effective for you with your own unique variations/adjustments as necessary.

To get started, create a routine by following the four-week daily practice located in My Daily Program section. Then evaluate the impact on your body. Using your evaluation, customize a weekly *Reaching Impossible Limits* program based on exercises that work for you. Success is in your hands.

The combination of the five pillars leads to extraordinary limitless results. If you are committed, nothing can stop you. Start now to become a stronger, slimmer, healthier, and faster top performer. Then share your results and customized programs on social media.

Chapter 2

Let's Do It

Before starting the *Reaching Impossible Limits* method for four weeks, start with the quick and easy changes below that will be explained in detail in the following chapters.

- Tape your Mouth - Chapter 12

  Be aware of how you breathe. Tape your mouth on a daily basis for a couple of hours to check if you breathe through the nose or mouth.

- Room Temperature - Chapter 19

  Stop heating your residence too much by gradually decreasing the temperature of your house to $18°C$ ($64°F$).

- Physical Exercises - Chapter 21

  Select a physical activity you want to practice three times a week. Swimming or yoga is advised. (Consult your medical practitioner, however, before practicing any breathing exercises or physical exercises.)

You can explore the book, exercises, and science for deeper insight. You can also directly begin practicing the program located in My Daily Program section. Each exercise of the *Reaching Impossible* method is explained and deconstructed in this book. Readers who learn best visually will have the opportunity to watch videos.

Part B

Pillar 1 – Mental Fortitude

Free Your Unbelievable Mind Power

Chapter 3 - Your Three Minds

How your minds interact between each other
│ 391 words │ 6 minutes' reading time │ 17 minutes' video time │

Chapter 4 - Changing Your Feelings and Beliefs

Your most enslaving prison is the jail of your beliefs
│ 551 words │ 6 minutes' reading time │ 29 minutes' video time │

Chapter 5 - The Power of Visualization

Achievement of your most unthinkable goals
│ 386 words │ 4 minutes' reading time │ 25 minutes' video time │

Chapter 6 - The Power of Incantations

Your best and easiest friend to succeed
│ 221 words │ 1 minutes' reading time │ 8 minutes' video time │

Chapter 3

Your Three Minds

Most of us don't know that we have the most powerful self-improvement tool available to us immediately and for free—our mind. When fully controlling the mind, we become a stronger, slimmer, healthier, and faster top performer.

René Descartes' infamous statement, "I think, therefore, I am," is overly simplistic. To understand the mind's complexity, let's break it down into three parts, using illustrations:

> Let's say you are the CEO (*conscious mind*) of a 100,000-employee technology company. As CEO, you are responsible to give orders and directions to your executive team (*subconscious mind*). Your executive team then decides if the orders and directions need to be delegated to their respective teams (*unconscious mind*), depending on the complexity of the request. Finally, if the orders/directions are delegated, your executives (*subconscious mind*) must collect and combine the information from their respective teams (*unconscious mind*) to provide you (*conscious mind*) a high-level summary.

> Let's continue this example to identify how the knowledge is split between the three minds:

> As a CEO (*conscious mind*), you are the voice and the face of your company. The public and media know only you. You have general knowledge of the company, so you do not need to know more than 10 percent of the subject matter. If you

have questions about the value of the lending portfolio in the past months, for example, you email your Chief Risk Officer (*subconscious mind*). He can reply right away to 50 to 60 percent of your questions.

For the other 30 to 40 percent of the questions, your Chief Risk Officer (*subconscious mind*) will email his lending risk teams (*unconscious mind*) for an answer because he cannot accurately remember historical values.

Then, your Chief Risk Officer (*subconscious mind*) will email you (*conscious mind*) a summarized answer.

This story and the roles of our three minds are visually explained in the next pages.

The CEO Example

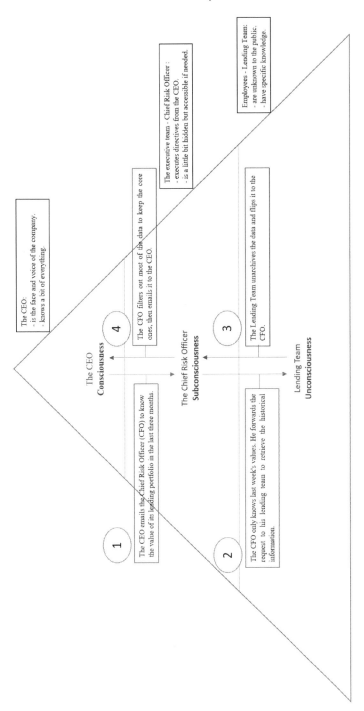

The CEO:
- is the face and voice of the company.
- knows a bit of everything.

The executive team - Chief Risk Officer :
- executes directives from the CEO.
- is a little bit hidden but accessible if needed.

Employees - Lending Team:
- are unknown to the public.
- have specific knowledge.

The CFO filters out most of the data to keep the core ones, then emails it to the CEO.

The Lending Team unarchives the data and flips it to the CFO.

The CEO
Consciousness

The Chief Risk Officer
Subconsciousness

Lending Team
Unconsciousness

The CEO emails the Chief Risk Officer (CFO) to know the value of its lending portfolio in the last three months.

The CFO only knows last week's values. He forwards the request to his lending team to retrieve the historical information.

1

2

3

4

The Three Minds

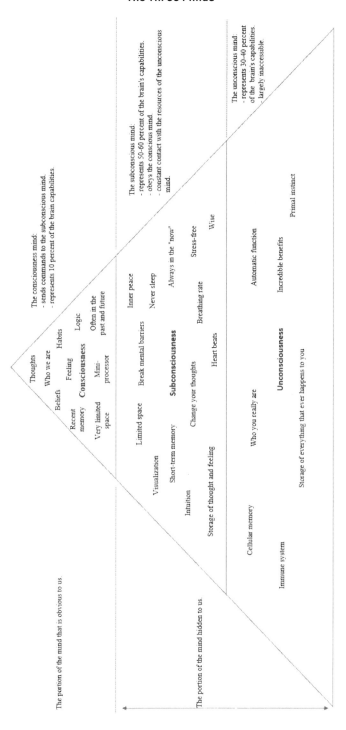

The portion of the mind that is obvious to us.

The consciousness mind:
- sends commands to the subconscious mind.
- represents 10 percent of the brain capabilities.

The subconscious mind:
- represents 50-60 percent of the brain's capabilities.
- obeys the conscious mind.
- constant contact with the resources of the unconscious mind.

The unconscious mind:
- represents 30–40 percent of the brain's capabilities, largely inaccessible.

The portion of the mind hidden to us.

Beliefs

Thoughts

Who we are

Feeling

Habits

Logic

Recent memory

Consciousness

Mini-processor

Often in the past and future

Very limited space

Limited space

Break mental barriers

Inner peace

Never sleep

Always in the "now"

Stress-free

Visualization

Subconsciousness

Wise

Short-term memory

Change your thoughts

Breathing rate

Intuition

Heart beats

Storage of thought and feeling

Cellular memory

Who you really are

Unconsciousness

Automatic function

Incredible benefits

Primal instinct

Immune system

Storage of everything that ever happens to you

As shown in the representation above, your history never disappears from your body. Even if less than one percent of the information that flows through the brain reaches your conscious awareness, you have access to the rest of your history through the unconscious and subconscious minds.

Fact: under hypnosis, people have the ability to remember events that have happened in the past. It is an effective method to bring back memories and solve traumas.

Resources

- Book

  Mind Power into the 21st Century: Techniques to Harness the Astounding Powers of Thought, John Kehoe

- Online Reading

  www.sciencedirect.com/topics/neuroscience/hypnosis

- Video

  TED Talk, *How your brain constructs reality*, Anil Seth

Chapter 4

Changing Your Feelings and Beliefs

Why am I anxious or jealous or self-confident right now? These adjectives are only thoughts, at a specific moment, that are based on internal representation of your beliefs, life experiences, and emotions.

The Three Principles model, founded by Sydney Banks, explains how the mind, consciousness, and thought interact to create feelings.

The Three Principles model

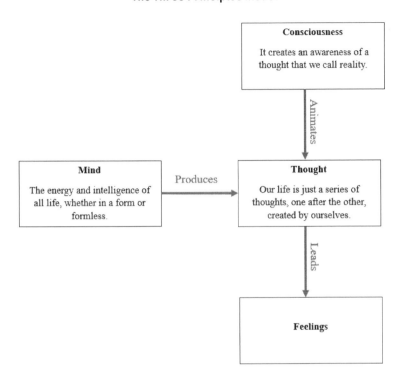

As highlighted in the model, feelings are not caused by external events or people but by the interpretation of thoughts. Therefore, working on how you interpret your thoughts can lead to freedom from stress, judgments, and limited thinking.

Never say you can't do something. Never say you can't be rich. Never say you are anxious. "Never" thoughts are created only by your own making and reality. Limiting beliefs put a cap on your performance and successes.

The key is to change your thinking through developing an appropriate consciousness by directing your thoughts. Whatever you are experiencing now has been customized solely for you by your mind.

Use your mind rather than letting your mind use you, and thus change the way you see yourself. For example, you can reverse your beliefs:

From	To
Uncomfortable - I can't jump in cold water.	Comfortable - I immerse in cold water for 30 seconds.
Not smart - I can't be rich.	Prosperity - I develop and monetize a unique skill.
No Leadership - I can't be a leader.	Empowerment - I improve my communication skills to influence people.

Exercise

Spend five minutes per day transforming a negative belief into a positive belief.

1. Step 1 - Select a negative belief.

   Ex: I am uncomfortable talking to strangers.

2. Step 2 - Transfer your negative belief to a positive belief.

   Today, I will talk to two random people at the gym about their training programs.

3. Step 3 - Daily work on your new positive belief.

   After successfully talking to random people in a controlled environment (e.g., at the gym), you are now empowered. You reproduce the same exercise in a non-controlled environment (e.g., in the street). The belief will slowly move from uncomfortable to comfortable.

4. Step 4 - Acknowledge and pay attention to your thousands of thoughts; regardless of whether they are positive or negative.

   Ex: Even if I am unable to talk to a stranger now, I acknowledge my negative belief.

5. Step 5 - Succeeding in transforming a negative belief into a positive belief will automatically lead to questioning other self-imposed beliefs.

   Ex: After a couple weeks of practicing small talk at the gym, I am now able to converse with strangers in the street. There is no more limitation on my ability to talk to strangers.

Keep in mind

If the subconscious mind has picked up negativity such as "I am not a creative person," it will consider the negative belief to be true. In this example, you won't ever be creative. Your mind will bring thoughts and situations to confirm your beliefs whether true or not.

"If you want to know what your thoughts were like in the past, look at your body today. If you want to know what your body will be like in the future, look at your thoughts today" (author unknown). Knowing and recognizing that you are your own reality-maker is the pivotal point in changing your beliefs and feelings.

Resources

- Online Course

    UDEMY, *NLP Practioner Certification*, Kain Ramsay and Steven Burns

- Videos

    TED Talk, *Do we see reality as it is*, Donald Hoffman

    YouTube, *How to change a belief | Tony Robbins*

Chapter 5

The Power of Visualization

Every morning, as soon as I wake up, I visualize my goal below. It provides me the strength and the ideas to reach it.

> *I have talked about* Reaching Impossible Limits *in front of hundreds of thousands of people during workshops and seminars. My events have always been fully booked in just a couple of minutes.*

> *As a speaker, I have been booked two years in advance around the world. Billions of people have listened to my interviews, watched my podcasts, and bought my book.*

> *I have received millions of amazing reviews and praises about my book and method. I feel proud of my impact on society. I have a sense of accomplishment.*

I only recently developed the *Reaching Impossible Limits* methodology and wrote this book. I nevertheless daily practice the power of visualization to reach my goals. Successful people, especially athletes, often practice visualizing their goals. Muhammad Ali, a boxing legend, used to constantly stress the power of seeing himself victorious before a fight.

How Visualization Works

When I arrived in Toronto in 2012, I was biking across the city to visit. As I stopped at the red traffic light, I looked at the building on my right and said, "I want to live in that building." I visualized myself living there. The building met all my criteria such as being in a quiet area, no obstructed view, close to downtown, in front of a park, and having a view of the lake.

I thought it would be impossible to buy in this building, but every day I visualized myself purchasing a unit. Then, in 2017, I was looking across the city to buy a condo. Guess what? The second apartment I visited was the one I had been visualizing daily, and it was located in this building.

Characteristics Developed by Visualization

- Building your internal motivation to succeed
- Increasing positive thoughts
- Programing your subconscious mind to generate creative ideas, and finding unknown resources
- Reducing stress

Exercise

Practice the following three-step visualization process twice daily:

1. Identify a goal that you believe and accept. Provide as many details as possible.
2. Practice deep relaxation until your mind is quiet.
3. Visualize Step 1 as if you have already achieved it.

The power of visualization can also be reinforced with Emotional Freedom Techniques (refer to Chapter 9).

Resources

- Videos

   YouTube, *The Power of Visualization* by The Best of Masters

   YouTube, *Lewis Pugh swims the North Pole*

Chapter 6

The Power of Incantations

A tremendous number of scientific studies have demonstrated that whatever you believe will happen to you. If you think you will get the flu this year, for example, your chances of getting it will increase.

Once a belief has formed, you will reject any information that contradicts it, by filtering for what you want to hear. The key is to change your beliefs from your subconscious mind.

The power of repeating an affirmation while using your body and voice influences the thoughts that are occurring in your mind. Even if you do not initially believe what you affirm, after a four-minute practice twice a day for three months, you will believe it.

That is why after repeating again and again a story in their mind, people tend to believe that story happened even if it did not. It is called the "illusory truth effect."

Exercise

Simply say aloud every morning and evening in front a mirror what you want your beliefs to be. As an example, I repeat twice a day the following affirmations:

- Every day I am getting better and better in every way.

- I attract the greatest people and the best circumstances.

- I celebrate my victories today.

- My body is a healing mechanism. I always feel great.

- There are limitless opportunities for me in every aspect of my life.

Resources

- Video

  YouTube, *Tony Robbins - The Power of Incantations vs. Affirmations*

Part C

Pillar 2 – Concentration

The power of Meditation

Chapter 7 - Meditation
Unlock your full potential
│ 896 words │ 5 minutes' reading time │ 35 minutes' video time │

Chapter 8 - Bhramari Pranayama
The incredible power of sound
│ 342 words │ 2 minutes' reading time │ 2 minutes' video time │

Chapter 9 - Emotional Freedom Technique
Resolve your mental game
│ 540 words │ 6 minutes' reading time │ 4 minutes' video time │

Chapter 7

Meditation

I have had the opportunity to try different meditation methods, ranging from breath awareness meditation to transcendental meditation. When focusing on the mind, we conserve energies and do not dissipate them through irrelevant activities. The mind gets a chance to reset itself to an unexcited state even after only a couple of minutes when closing our eyes. The body responds with a significant decrease in blood pressure, heart rate, and breathing rate.

Meditation is the most efficient exercise to develop our power of concentration and to perform the delicate task of introspection. Hundreds of scientific research papers stress how meditation can help control the autonomic nervous system.

One the most challenging trainings I have ever tried, and also the most rewarding one, is the Vipassana meditation. The experience left me speechless. If you ask me, "Where do I start so that I can *Reach Impossible Limits*," I will recommend a daily practice of the Vipassana meditation.

What Is Vipassana?

To clarify upfront, there is no religion or ritual associated with the Vipassana method. Vipassana is different from mindfulness meditation or transcendental meditation, which respectively focus on awareness or mantras. It dictates that you see things as they really are through the exploration of the depths of the mind by means of body sensations. Non-reaction to whatever sensations you feel, even if they hurt, is the end goal.

The Vipassana technique may be learned through a ten-day residential course in an official center. Once the course starts, you must follow strict rules: no talking, no interaction with others, no phone, no reading, and so on …

I had read a lot about how Vipassana improves your well-being, efficiency, and performance, by working on mind and body. One day, I decided to register to create my own opinion from personal experience.

A month before starting the retreat, I read the rules again. I thought I would not be able to follow or handle them, so I cancelled my registration, finding any kind of non-valid excuses to support my decision. I was also thinking, *I am a non-religious person with no major issue; why do I need to attend a ten-day retreat?* This happened twice.

A couple of months later, I registered for the third time and attended a ten-day silent meditation retreat in June 2018 in Toronto. I was really impressed by the organization. Volunteers cook and clean for participants. For ten days, we didn't do anything—strictly nothing.

Except for one key element—meditation. We woke up at 4 a.m. each morning and meditated eleven hours per day. We eat two meals per day (and the food was great). Each evening, we attended a ninety-minute debriefing of the day, followed by bedtime at 10 p.m.

Sitting for such a long time without moving teaches the mind how to remain calm and equanimous no matter how pleasant or unpleasant the self-sensation may be.

My Results

At the end of the ten-day program, participants had the opportunity to talk to one another. One participant, who was an athlete, said his performance significantly improves after each retreat, even if he has not trained and moved for more than ten days each time. I really believe him because my own results have been well above my expectations.

First, my capacity to concentrate, my decision-making skills, and my confidence level have significantly increased because I have trained my mind to live in the now. I would not have been able to create and write *Reaching Impossible Limits* before this experience.

Second, I fully understand that no matter the pain (as I sat for ten hours a day) or the situation, I do not need to react.

Third, I have developed better introspection regarding the reasons my mind is chattering in stressful situations. I now have the capacity to quickly quiet it.

Last, I have significantly increased my brain neuroplasticity, which is the brain's ability to generate new neural connections in response to new information, sensory stimulation, development, or damage. Regeneration of your brain cells is the key to staying younger and healthier.

Practice
Unveil your hidden mind super-power capacity and mental abilities through a daily practice of meditation.

Exercise 1 - Vipassana meditation
Start with a five-minute daily meditation practice. Increase your meditation time by one minute per week, using the following steps:

1. Find a quiet space where you can sit comfortably.
2. Close your eyes.
3. Make no effort to control the breath; simply breathe naturally.
4. Focus on the sensations of your breath; it will help your mind to stay focused.
5. Whenever you are distracted, first acknowledge the distraction and then return to focusing on the sensations of your breath.

If you can, register for a ten-day Vipassana course.

Exercise 2 - Body-scan meditation
The body-scan meditation is an easy and accessible relaxation technique. Practice daily, from a couple of minutes up to forty-five minutes, especially after a workout, to analyze and relax your body.

1. Lie down on your back. Be comfortable.
2. Close your eyes. (Do not fall asleep. This is not a napping exercise.)
3. Bring awareness to the body, breathing in and out.
4. Scan your entire body.

Begin scanning your body, starting from the top of your head and moving down to embrace each part of your body until you scan your toes. Keep your attention focused on each part of your body.

Resources

- Book

  Full Catastrophe Living, Jon Kabat-Zinn

- Online Readings

  https://www.dhamma.org/en-US/index

  https://eocinstitute.org/meditation/10-key-brain-regions-up-graded-with-meditation-2/

- Videos

  YouTube, *How to Practice Vipassana Meditation in 5 minutes*

  YouTube, *Body Scan Meditation - Jon Kabat-Zinn*

Chapter 8

Bhramari Pranayama

What Is Bhramari Pranayama?
Known as "humming breath" or "bee breath" in English, Bhramari pranayama is the action of making a light humming sound while practicing breathing exercises.

Benefits
There are so many incredible benefits of practicing the humming breath, such as reducing fatigue, calming the mind, and/or improving concentration. Among these benefits, there is one that will improve your health; when exhaling through the nose, the humming sound generates an increase in nitric oxide up to fifteen-fold compared to quiet exhalation.

Nitric Oxide (NO)
Nitric oxide (NO) is one of the most important molecules produced in the nasal cavity and the lining of blood vessels throughout your body. NO has the following benefits:

- Develops memory
- Helps the immune system fight against bacteria and tumours
- Improves sleep quality
- Increases endurance and strength

- Opens blood vessels ($\rightarrow$ increasing libido)
- Reduces inflammation
- Regulates blood pressure by dilating arteries

Practice

Practice Bhramari pranayama following these steps once daily:

1. Sit straight and comfortably.

2. Breathe normally and relax the whole body. Keep your eyes and mouth closed.

3. Plug both ears by gently placing your thumbs on the cartilage of your ears, but not inside.

4. Place your index fingers on your forehead, just above the eyebrows.

5. Place your middle, ring, and pinky fingers across the eyes so that the tips of the fingers press very gently against the bridge of the nose.

6. Take a long deep breath through both nostrils.

7. As you breathe out, gently press the cartilage while creating a continuous humming sound from the throat for as long as you can. Keep your mouth closed. The sound is similar to "Hmm" or the humming of a bee.

8. Repeat the above steps 5 times.

It's important that you practice this exercise with a closed mouth if you want to get nitric oxide benefits. "Nitric Oxide (NO) is released in the nasal airways in humans. During inspiration through the nose, this NO will follow the airstream to the lower airways and the lungs."

Resources

- Online Readings

  www.atsjournals.org/doi/abs/10.1164/rccm.200202-138BC

  https://thorax.bmj.com/content/54/10/947

- Video

  YouTube, *Yoga Exercise To Increase Concentration - Bhramari Pranayama (Humming Bee Breath)*

Chapter 9

Emotional Freedom Technique (EFT)

Do you want to quickly and efficiently implement positive goals, lose weight, relieve pain, find solutions to life challenges, resolve phobias, have more positive emotions, and stop your limiting beliefs?

Emotional Freedom Technique (EFT), or "Tapping," is a powerful technique to improve your physical health and emotional state. It can be used for almost everything. Professional athletes, for instance, use EFT to improve their performance.

Tapping works on your mental, emotional, and physical well-being at the same time through incorporating the power of the mind into "Western" medicine. EFT does not replace medical treatments.

How EFT Works from a Scientific Point of View

EFT is the same process as acupuncture but without the needles. Acupuncture has been used for over five thousand years. The tapping of nine primary meridian endpoints unblocks the energy channels (qi) into the organs. Tapping targets the root cause of symptoms in the body and mind by stopping the body's stress response.

When facing stressful situations, the body activates its defense mechanism to fight or flee by setting off the amygdala's (part of the limbic system's) fire alarm. Tapping meridian endpoints deactivates the amygdala by sending a calming response to the body. Any stressful situations will then be considered as "no big deal" by the hippocampus.

EFT is an Eight-Step Process
It only takes a couple of minutes to learn EFT, and it carries no risk.

Preparation steps

1. Identify your "Most Pressing Issue" (MPI)

   MPI Ex: I am afraid I will not able to engage the audience during my work presentation.

   Tip - Define your MPI as specifically as possible. Do not hide your negative feelings, because the goal of EFT is to neutralize them. Be sure to only target one issue at a time.

2. Define a reminder phrase

   The reminder phrase is a couple of words that bring to mind your MPI.

   Reminder phrase Ex: Public speaking is stressful.

3. Rate the intensity of your MPI

   Assign a number on a 0 to 10 scale (10 being the worst the issue gets and 0 being no problem whatsoever). The distress number will be your benchmark for evaluating your progress.

4. Write a setup statement

   The set-up statement is designed to acknowledge and accept your MPI.

   Setup Statement Ex: *Even though* [add your MPI from Step 1], *I deeply and completely accept myself.*

   The EFT preparation is now over.

Practice

5. Tap on the Karate Chop point

   Repeat your setup statement aloud 3 times while tapping the Karate Chop point (see location of tapping points at the end of this chapter).

6. Tap your 8 meridian endpoints

Tap 5 times on each of the following eight meridian points while repeating your reminder phrase:

1.) Top of Head

2.) Eyebrow

3.) Side of Eye

4.) Under Eye

5.) Under Nose

6.) Chin Point

7.) Collarbone

8.) Under Arm

Repeat Step 5 twice.

Tip - It does not matter which hand or the side of your body you use when tapping.

9. Take a deep breath

10. Rate your MPI again

11. Step 9 – Repeat

Repeat steps 4 through 9 until the intensity of your MPI has significantly decreased. Never bury your problems. Accepting, admitting, and addressing your MPI will lead to clearing it.

Resources

- Book

  The Tapping Solution, Nick Ortner

- Video

  YouTube, *How to Tap with Jessica Ortner: Emotional Freedom Technique Informational Video*

Location of Tapping Points

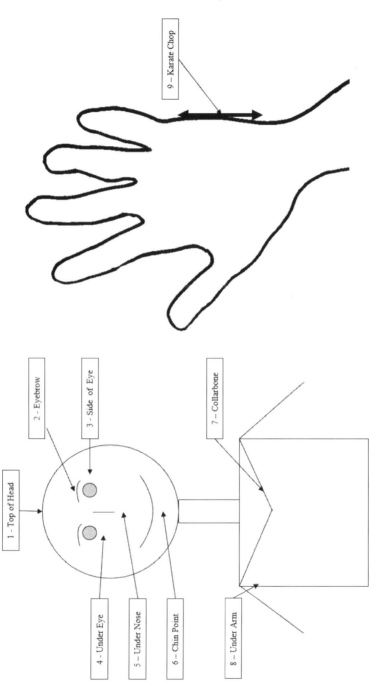

Part D

The Forgotten Breathing Facts and Science

Free Your Unbelievable Breath Power

Chapter 10 – Facts about Breathing
Unknown system
│ 311 words │ 2 minutes' reading time │

Chapter 11 - Mouth Breathing
My mouth, my problems
│ 402 words │ 4 minutes' reading time │ 9 minutes' video time │

Chapter 12 - Nose Breathing
So easy and basic, why didn't I know this?
│ 363 words │ 2 minutes' reading time │ 13 minutes' video times │

Chapter 13 -Visualization of the Respiratory System
How awesome you really are
│ 622 words │ 6 minutes' reading time │ 3 minutes' video times │

Chapter 10

Facts about Breathing

Interesting Facts About the Breath
Breathing Volume and Rate Facts

1. The breathing rate is faster in children and women than in men.

2. Healthy people inhale 4 to 6 litres (135 to 169 US fluid ounces) of air per minute generated by 10 to 12 breaths of 0.5 litres.

3. In the past 24 hours, you have taken approximately 17,000 breaths and breathed approximately 8,500 litres (287,419 US fluid ounces).

4. Panic attacks occur when a person breaths more than 20 L/min (676us fl oz/min).

5. Rapid breathing can lead to overeating and weight gain.

6. Overbreathing can lead to fatigue, dry mouth, stress, anxiety, dizziness, pain, asthma, and panic attacks.

Respiratory System Facts

7. Breathing is the only autonomous system of the body we can control.

8. Lungs are the only organs in the human body that float on water.

9. If lungs were open flat, they would cover the entire size of a tennis court.

10. Your right lung is slightly larger than your left lung, allowing room for your heart.

Breathing Chemical-Composition Facts

11. Breathing consumes half a litre of water a day and at least four times more when exercising. When breathing onto glass, this is the fog you see.

12. Breathing has very little to do with oxygen. Air is made up of 79 percent nitrogen and 21 percent oxygen.

13. The body exhales 75 percent nitrogen, 15 percent oxygen, 5 percent water vapor, and 5 percent carbon dioxide.

14. Seventy percent of body waste is eliminated through breathing, 20 percent though the skin, 7 percent via urine, and 3 percent through feces.

Breathing Effect Facts

15. Breath is an indicator of your emotions in the moment. Changing how you breathe can improve your mood.

16. Deep breaths lead to diminished performance.

17. Fitness performance is limited by breathlessness, not by your legs or arms.

Resources

- Online Reading

    http://amazingfacts4u.com/breathing/

Chapter 11

Mouth Breathing

Interesting Facts about Breathing Through the Mouth

Mouth breathing is

1. Synonymous with emergency, activating the fight-or-flight response.

2. Highly correlated to sleep apnea.

Mouth breathing leads to

3. A higher risk for cold symptoms, cavities, and gum disease.

4. Lower oxygen concentration in the blood, which can lead to higher blood pressure and heart failure.

Mouth breathing decreases

5. Productivity significantly, which can lead to

- Bad mood

- Low energy level

- Low levels of concentration

- More fatigue

Mouth breathing may generate

6. An increase in acidification, risk of cavities, and gum diseases stemming from a dry mouth.

7. Lisps and speech disorders the abnormal position of the tongue may cause.

Mouth breathing allows

8. The use of the upper chest, which results in rapid breathing or hypoventilation.

The Modern Human Face

The primary functions of the mouth are to communicate and eat, not to breathe.

Consequences of Mouth Breathing

1. Arched lower back.

2. Crooked nose.

3. Longer and narrower face. In fewer than 400 hundred years, the human face has moved to downward growth because of mouth breathing instead of keeping a straight-growth pattern as occurs with nose breathing.

4. Long-term stress on the neck, shoulders, and cervical structure.

5. Small lower jaw.

Reasons for Mouth Breathing

The move to a modern face has been explained by the change in human lifestyle, especially the nutrition component of the food we eat, and stress. Nowadays, diet is composed of about 95 percent acidic foods and 5 percent alkaline foods. It was the opposite hundreds of years ago.

Types of food

Types	Examples	pH ranges	Lead to
Acidic	Dairy products, processed foods, eggs, meat, grain, sodas, bread, tea, and alcohol	0.0 – 6.9	Overbreathing
Neutral	Butter and oil	7.0	
Alkaline	Fruits, nuts, legumes, vegetables, potatoes, plain yogurt, honey, chocolate, and water	7.1 – 14	Breathing-friendly

The pH value measures a substance's acidity or alkalinity. Your blood pH must stay between 7.36 and 7.44. Cells die when the pH is less than 6.8 or greater than 7.8.

Advice: Balance the type of food you eat. Your body will auto-regulate your pH level with the help of carbon dioxide (refer to chapter 15). Processed foods are not recommended.

It Is Not Too Late

If you don't already breathe primarily through your nose, it's not too late to switch to nose breathing. Go to the next chapter to learn how to breathe correctly.

Resources
- Online Readings

  https://www.drmommasays.com/healthcare/nose/truth-about-health-consequences-of-mouth-breathing/

  https://www.healthline.com/nutrition/the-alkaline-diet-myth#ph

- Videos

  YouTube, *The Story of Headgear*

  YouTube, *Mouth Breathing Changes your face*

Chapter 12

Nose Breathing

Interesting Facts about Nose Breathing

Nose breathing protects

1. Your body by filtering, humidifying, and warming or cooling the air (depending on the temperature) before it enters the lungs. Nose breathing reduces the probability of sore throats and even ear infections.

Nose breathing allows

2. The correct position of the tongue (against the upper palate) and lips (together), leading to natural dental arches and straight teeth.

3. The entire rib cage to breathe by engaging your twelve, paired ribs to act as levers that massage the heart and lungs, rather than acting as a cage that squeezes the heart and lungs.

4. More time for the lungs to extract oxygen from the air, because nostrils are smaller than the mouth, and air exhaled through the nose creates a backflow of air (and oxygen) into the lungs.

Nose breathing increases

5. Blood oxygen and carbon dioxide levels, lowering the breathing rate and improving overall lung volume.

6. The production of nitric oxide (refer to chapter 8).

Nose breathing reduces

7. Hypertension and stress, because nose breathing forces us to slow down.

8. Recovery times and improves endurance.

9. The number of breaths. This is a sign of better health (refer to part E).

Nose breathing helps to

10. Increase energy and vitality resulting from an increase in oxygen in cells (refer to chapter 15), and to experience better workouts.

11. Lower the heart rate.

12. Prevent overtraining.

The science behind these facts is explained in Part E.

Description of "Correct" Breathing

Unleash your untapped potential with a functional breathing pattern. The breath must have the following characteristics:

- Driven by the diaphragm
- Effortless
- Natural pause after exhalation
- Rhythmic/regular
- Through the nose

Practice

Developing a nose-breathing pattern is easy, accessible, and only takes three months.

1. Before going to bed, tape your mouth. It forces you into nose breathing through the night. If uncomfortable at first, start with a couple of hours during the day. I use 3M Micropore tape. Avoid this technique after drinking or eating, or if you feel sick.

2. You should be able to exercise with your mouth closed. If not, reduce the intensity of your workout.

Resources

- Online Readings

  https://www.lenus.ie/hse/bitstream/10147/559021/1/JAN15Art7.pdf

  https://lifespa.com/15-benefits-nose-breathing-exercise/

- Video

  YouTube, *Nose Breathing Benefits - Oxygen Advantage*

Chapter 13

Visualization of the Respiratory System

The following chapter provides a scientific overview of how breathing works.
Learning how the respiratory system works leads to a deeper understanding of the various methods outlined in this book. (If you want to bypass the scientific aspect, proceed to the next chapter.)

Respiratory System

The breathing cycle includes two main processes:

- Inhalation - the active process of intake of air into the lungs.

- Exhalation - the passive process of letting air out from the lungs.

Inhaling Breath Cycle

When breathing in, the air follows a complex process throughout our body:

1. The diaphragm contracts.

2. Air rushes in through the nose and mouth into the main air passage.

3. The oxygen heads down through the pharynx, the larynx, and then the trachea, which filters the air.

4. The bronchi split the air between the two lungs.

5. The oxygen reaches the alveoli.

6. The oxygen enters the blood through the tiny capillaries surrounding the alveoli.

7. After absorbing oxygen, the red blood cells leave the lungs with the help of a protein called hemoglobin.

8. The oxygen is carried to your heart.

9. The heart then pumps the oxygenated blood through all the cells and organs in your body.

Exhaling Breath Cycle

As body cells consume glucose (from food breakdown) and oxygen, water vapor and carbon dioxide respectively are produced.

1. Cells release carbon dioxide and water back into the bloodstream.

2. Red blood cells pick up carbon dioxide and waste.

3. Red blood cells come back through the capillaries into the lungs.

4. Carbon dioxide and waste enter the alveoli.

5. Carbon dioxide and waste are in your lungs from your blood vessels.

6. The diaphragm relaxes upward into its resting domed shape. The space inside your chest gets smaller.

7. Carbon dioxide and waste are breathed out through the reverse process from bronchioles to the nose.

Roles of Respiratory Organs

Let's get a better understanding of the respiratory system process when inhaling.

Inhaling	Description	Function
Diaphragm	This main respiratory muscle is located below the lungs.	Contracts and flattens out. It creates a vacuum effect that pulls air into the lungs.
Nose	Air enters through the two nostrils.	Warms, moisturizes, and filters air entering the body.
Mouth	Air can also enter through the mouth.	Supplements your nose.
Pharynx	This is the throat.	Allows air to pass through it while keeping food and drink from blocking the airway.
Larynx	The voice box—the portion of the respiratory tract containing the vocal cords, which produce sound.	Protects the trachea by producing a strong cough reflex if any solid objects pass through the throat.
Trachea	This is your windpipe.	Lets the air flow into the lungs. It traps dust and other dirt particles through its wall.
Bronchi	Extension of the trachea through its division into two tubes—one entering the left lung and one entering the right lung.	Highways for gas exchange, with oxygen going to the lungs (and carbon dioxide leaving the lungs through them when exhaling).
Bronchioles	Bronchi, the main airways, branch off into smaller and smaller passageways, the smallest of which are called bronchioles—30,000 of them in each lung.	Form a tree structure in the lungs so that air reaches every corner to be supplied to each alveolus.

Inhaling	Description	Function
Lungs	Two spongy air-filled organs in our chest, located on either side of the chest (thorax).	Help oxygen from the air we breathe enter the red cells in the blood.
Alveoli	About 600 million are in your lungs.	Allow oxygen from the air to pass through the wall of each alveolus into the bloodstream through capillaries (blood vessels).
Heart	Part of the circulatory system, not the respiratory system.	Works with veins, arteries, and capillaries to transport blood throughout the body.

Resources

- Online Reading

  https://www.britannica.com/science/
  human-respiratory-system#ref66123

- Video

  YouTube, *What Happens When You Breathe? How The Lungs Work Animation*

Part E

Pillar 3 - Breathing

Understand Your Unbelievable Breath Power

Chapter 14 - Take a Deep Breath
Let's feel great
| 245 words | 1 minutes' reading time |

Chapter 15 - Carbon Dioxide Is Very Useful
My friend
| 727 words | 4 minutes' reading time | 3 minutes' video time |

Chapter 16 - My Breath Analysis
First thing of my day
| 548 words | 3 minutes' reading time | 2 minutes' video time |

Chapter 17 - Process to Feel Great
My body feels
| 185 words | 1 minute' reading time | 4 minutes' video time |

Chapter 18 - Be an Athlete
Developing unique capacities
| 565 words | 3 minutes' reading time | 20 minutes' video time |

Chapter 14

Take a Deep Breath

In the following two chapters, we will clarify common misconceptions about oxygen. Then we will move to breathing techniques to becoming a stronger, slimmer, healthier, and faster top performer.

Misconception 1: Taking a larger breath improves performance through an increase in oxygen.

Oxygen saturation (SpO$_2$) definition

SpO$_2$, an indicator of oxygen transport in the body, indicates if sufficient oxygen is being supplied to the body, especially to the lungs. More specifically, it is the percentage of oxygenated hemoglobin compared to the total amount of hemoglobin in the blood.

Normal SpO2 values

Normal blood oxygen levels in the human body are considered 95 to 99 percent. Try to measure your SpO$_2$ at any time with a pulse oximeter. Meet your medical practitioner if your SpO$_2$ is below 95 percent. On the other hand, 100 percent is almost not possible.

True or False? Since oxygen, or O$_2$, is the fuel used by our muscles to work efficiently, our performance should technically increase with larger breaths.

False: In fact, we won't increase the oxygen saturation (SpO_2) because the blood is almost always already saturated in oxygen at 95 to 99 percent.

A larger breath does not improve performance, because the body does not need to inhale more oxygen.

Consequences of Taking Large Breaths

1. Taking larger breathes has no benefits on your performance other than feeling great.

2. Larger breaths reduce oxygenation and performance even further because of the removal of too much CO_2 (refer to chapter 15).

Resources

- Online Reading

  https://www.normalbreathing.com/Articles-breathing-maximum-brain-oxygenation.php

Chapter 15

Carbon Dioxide Is Very Useful

Misconception 2: The need for oxygen is a critical factor on respiratory rate.

Regulation of Breathing

Respiration is controlled by the autonomic nervous system within the medulla oblongata (considered to be "the boss") in the brain. Its main function is to send signals to the muscles that control respiration to cause breathing with the help of chemoreceptors.

Chemoreceptors are specialized sensory receptors that monitor the change in concentration of oxygen, carbon dioxide, and blood pH level. They transmit this information to the autonomic nervous system. That's why our breathing constantly changes without us noticing.

The Bohr Effect

The Bohr Effect is a key concept for *Reaching Impossible Limits*. This counterintuitive effect can be summarized as follows:

1. Oxygen comes into the blood. (Keep in mind, your blood is already fully saturated with oxygen.)

2. Hemoglobin picks up the oxygen.

3. The oxygen is securely stored within the hemoglobin.

4. Carbon dioxide releases the oxygen from your hemoglobin by loosening the hemoglobin grip. This is key. **You need CO_2 to release O_2.**

5. Oxygen flows through tissues and organs.

If carbon dioxide concentration is low, oxygen is held tightly on the red blood cells. It makes you feel out of breath, and you overbreathe as a result.

Eliminating or Keeping CO_2

Even if the primary stimulus for breathing is to eliminate carbon dioxide, we need to keep the right amount of carbon dioxide in our body to unload oxygen from red blood cells to our organs and tissues.

The solution to this is nose breathing. Nose breathing reduces the number of breaths per minute, which in turn leads to keeping more carbon dioxide in our body. (Note: Carbon dioxide reacts with water to form carbonic acid; therefore, an increase in CO_2 results in a decrease in blood pH.)

Bohr Effect Process Flow Scenarios

Let's analyze the breathing process flow for the following scenarios:

- *Scenario 1* - There is too much carbon dioxide in my blood because I am holding my breath for thirty seconds. It needs to be breathed out.

- *Scenario 2* - The physical exercise is too intense; I am out of breath. As such, I am taking deep breaths.

- *Scenario 3* - I had a great day and ate mostly acidic food (see chapter 11). My pH level has decreased.

Result: The surplus of carbon dioxide or the lack of oxygen or the low pH level (scenarios 1, 2, and 3 respectively) trigger a deeper and faster breathing response. This overbreathing leads to a decrease in carbon dioxide within the body that results in an increase in pH level. We become more breathless because less oxygen is released to the muscles.

- *Scenario 4* - I spent the day at the farm and ate mostly alkaline food (see chapter 11). My pH level has increased.

Result: The high pH level triggers a lower-need-for breathing response. This underbreathing leads to an increase in carbon dioxide within the body that results in a decrease in pH level. There is less need to breathe because more oxygen is released to the muscles.

Carbon Dioxide, My Best Friend

To summarize, carbon dioxide performs the following functions:

- Regulates blood pH level
- Releases oxygen from red blood cells to your organs and tissues
- Vasodilates blood vessels

True or False?

False: In fact, the need for carbon dioxide is a critical factor on respiratory rate.

Key Life Conclusions

1. Stop breathing too much
2. Tape your mouth at night
3. Keep in mind:

- *Vicious cycle:* An increase in breathing leads to the exhalation of more carbon dioxide. This results in a decrease in carbon dioxide within the body. Less oxygen is then released to the organs and muscles. The vicious circle starts because the body needs to breathe more to get more oxygen. The automatic and easiest way to absorb more oxygen is breathing through the mouth (refer to chapter 11).

- *Virtuous cycle:* A decrease in breathing leads to the exhalation of less carbon dioxide. This results in an increase in carbon dioxide within the body. More oxygen is then released to the organs and muscles. The virtuous circle starts because the body is fully oxygenated. Therefore, there is less of a need to breathe. The automatic and easiest way to absorb less oxygen is breathing through the nose (refer to chapter 12).

Let's now learn new techniques to improve and develop our breathing.

Resources

- Online Reading

  https://www.livestrong.com/
  article/108342-factors-affect-respiration-rate/

- Video

  YouTube, *Oxygen Dissociation Curve Explained - Bohr Effect*

Chapter 16

My Breath Analysis

The Oxygen Advantage Method

Patrick McKeown, creator of the *Oxygen Advantage* method (built on *The Buteyko* method), has developed a series of breathing exercises based on the following scientific analysis during an intense workout.

- The consumption of oxygen increases, leading to a slightly reduced concentration of O_2 in the blood.

- Simultaneously, increased muscle activity and metabolic rate generates more carbon dioxide, leading to an increased concentration of CO_2 in the blood.

The only way to reduce the impact of breathing is to increase your tolerance to

- A higher concentration of CO_2.

- A lower concentration of O_2.

Maximal Oxygen Uptake—VO$_2$

VO_2 max, a performance-related metric, is the measure of the maximum amount of oxygen your body can utilize during a one-minute intense exercise.

A higher tolerance of CO_2 increases the delivery of O_2 that leads to a higher VO_2. Your breathlessness is lower because your body produces less effort.

Wake-up Exercise

Control Pause Test (CP) or *Body Oxygen Level Test* (BOLT) measures the length of time that you can comfortably hold your breath; it determines your sensitivity to carbon dioxide.

Practice

As soon you wake up, follow the steps below to measure your BOLT. It provides a daily accurate feedback on your health and breathing progress. You will need a stopwatch or cellphone.

1. Sit straight without crossing your legs, and breathe comfortably and gently.

2. After a gentle and normal exhalation, pinch your nose with your fingers to prevent air from entering your lungs. Start your stopwatch.

3. Time how many seconds until you feel *the first* desire to breathe. Keep in mind that BOLT is not a measurement of how long you can hold your breath.

4. Stop the watch, release your nose, and resume normal breathing. If you need to take a big breath, it means that you have held your breath for too long and the reading is inaccurate.

BOLT Results Analysis

If your BOLT score is 10 or below, meet an *Oxygen Advantage* instructor before practicing (refer to the resource section to find an instructor). A higher BOLT score means a higher tolerance to CO_2 which leads to a lower need for breathing.

BOLT Score in seconds	Breath	Symptoms	Type of breathing
10 and under	Heavy, irregular, noisy, and effortful.	Constant health issues → short life-expectancy.	Chest breathing and mouth-breathing. 15–30 breaths/min
20	Heavy but regular.	Average health → blocked nose, snoring, insomnia, coughing, short breath, and asthma.	Mouth-breathing. 15–20 breaths/min
30	Light, regular, calm, and effortless.	Good health → symptoms above may occur.	Nose-breathing. 10–15 breaths/min
40 and more	Light, regular, calm, and effortless.	Great health → feel great.	Nose-breathing. 6–10 breaths/min

Let's achieve a BOLT of at least 40 seconds to *Reach Impossible Limits*.

BOLT Key Information

- *Influencing Factors.* Your BOLT score is influenced by your health situation. Don't be discouraged. Whatever your health situation, the method includes breathing exercises to move forward.

- *Feeling Better.* You feel better each time your BOLT score increases by 5 seconds.

- *Physical Exercises.* Combining breathing exercises with physical exercise is the way to improve your BOLT score from 20 to 40.

- *Slowing down.* Slowing down your breathing is the most efficient exercise to work on the two variables of breathing—breathing volume and breathing rate.

Resources

- Book

  The Oxygen Advantage, Patrick McKeown

- Online Reading

  https://buteykoclinic.com/
  breathing-exercise-1-the-control-pause-part-i/

- Video

  YouTube, *How To Measure Your Control Pause?*

- Certified Instructors

  https://oxygenadvantage.com/instructors/

Chapter 17

Process to Feel Great

The *Oxygen Advantage* method is a three-step program incorporated in the *Reaching Impossible Limits* method. As stated by the ancient Chinese philosopher Lao Tzu, the human breath should be silent: "The perfect man breathes as if he does not breathe."

1. **Observe your breathing throughout the day**

   Goal: Stop losses of carbon dioxide.

   Always ask yourself: Is my breathing light, regular, unheard, and effortless in the moment?

   Solutions:

   - Close your mouth. Breathe through your nose day and night. Tape your mouth at night.
   - Stop big breathing: slow down and stop talking when your breathing becomes larger and deeper.
   - Be aware when sighing and yawning. When either occur, you lose carbon dioxide. Hold your breath for 5 to 10 seconds to compensate.

2. **Step 2 - Improve Tolerance for Carbon Dioxide**

   Goal: Reduce your breathing volume toward normal.

   Solution: Practice breathing techniques designed to maximize muscle oxygenation and energy production (refer to next chapter).

3. **Step 3 - Simulate High-Altitude Training**

   Goal: Increase oxygen capacity.

   Solution: Practice breathing techniques that simulate high-altitude training and increase your blood's carrying ability (refer to next chapter).

Resources

- Video

  YouTube, *Summary of Benefits of Oxygen Advantage program* by Patrick McKeown

Chapter 18

Be an Athlete

Efficient Exercises

Your daily BOLT score determines which combination of breathing exercises you can practice. The higher your BOLT score, the higher the number of available exercises.

General Safety Guidance

Some safety guidance before starting:

- Practice exercises that fit your BOLT score.

- Do not eat or drink (other than water) at least two hours before practicing.

- When resuming your normal breathing through the nose, your breathing must remain in control. If not, it means you pushed too hard.

Training Recommendation

As you will see in the next section, most of these exercises can be practiced anywhere, even at work. No one will notice you are working on your breathing.

I like to walk to work on a daily basis (even in the winter when the temperature is -20°C). It is a thirty-five-minute walk each way. I use that time to practice the Nose Unblocking Exercise, Breathe Light Walking, and Simulate High Altitude.

Exercises

The table below explains how and which exercises you can practice, depending on your BOLT score. If you want results, you need to practice breathing exercises daily that match your BOLT score.

	Breathing Recovery	Breathe Light	Nose Unblocking	Simulate High Altitude Training
Minimum BOLT to practice (in seconds)	BOLT > 10	BOLT > 15	BOLT > 20	BOLT > 25
Description	Great exercise to warm up and cool down before and after a workout.	Slow down your breathing to create a tolerable need for air.	Most efficient exercise to clear your nose. If your nose is clean, skip it.	Simulate the beneficial effects of high-altitude training and high-intensity training.
Duration	3 daily sets of 5 minutes.	3 daily sets of 10 minutes.	3 daily sets of 5 repetitions.	3 weekly sets of 10 repetitions.
Steps	1- Comfortably sit. 2- Small breath in and small breath out. 3- Gently exhale. 4- Pinch your nose. 5- Hold breath after a small breath out for 3-5 seconds. 6- Breathe normally for 10 seconds. 7- Repeat until calm.	1- Normal breaths through your nose. 2- Place one hand on your chest and one hand just above your navel. The hand on your chest should not move. 3- As you breathe, take shorter and shorter slow breaths to reduce the breath. 4- Resume normal breathing when the need for air is not tolerable.	1- Small breath in and small breath out. 2- Gently exhale. 3- Pinch your nose. 4- As you walk, hold your breath as long as you can. If you sit, move your shoulders from left to right to generate carbon dioxide. 5- Resume normal breathing through your nose. 6- Normal breathing for 1 minute.	1- Walk for 1 minute. 2- Gently exhale. 3- Pinch your nose. 4- Walk again, hold your breath until you feel a medium hunger for air. 5- Minimal breathing for 15 seconds while walking. 6- Normally breathe for 30 seconds.

	Breathing Recovery	Breathe Light	Nose Unblocking	Simulate High Altitude Training
YouTube	*Buteyko Breathing Method - Stop Asthma Attack, Panic Attack or Hyperventilation Attack.*	*Light Breathing Exercises - by Patrick McKeown*	*Unblock Your Nose Instantly by Simply Holding Your Breath*	*Simulate Altitude Training - Oxygen Advantage*
Comments	1- Practice 1 set when you wake up, 1 set in the afternoon, and 1 set at night. 2- BOLT > 10, you can replace sitting by slow walking.	1- Do NOT hold the breath. 2- BOLT > 20, practice it while walking or running.		1- BOLT > 30, practicing while running.

Part F

Pillar 4 - Cold Exposure

Beyond the Impossible

Chapter 19

Amazing Benefits

The *Reaching Impossible Limits* method incorporates cold exposure exercises for becoming a stronger, slimmer, healthier, and faster top performer. The goal of Pillar 4 is to strengthen the immune system and develop unbreakable mental fortitude.

Human biology needs good stress to trigger an avalanche of physiological responses that skip the conscious mind. Cold exposure is the perfect good-stress exercise to accomplish this. It will trigger four main components of your body:

1. Warming the body

2. Heightening mental awareness

3. Tweaking insulin production

4. Tightening the circulatory system

Science of Cold Exposure

Cold exposure, researched by scientific institutes, generates an increase in cortisol in the blood that leads to a significant decrease of inflammatory proteins. That's why athletes use cold baths and cryotherapy; it improves their recovery time and reduces the risk of injury.

Researchers have also demonstrated that regular cold exposure leads to an increase in white blood cells. These are the cells of the immune system that fight infection and diseases.

Benefits of Cold Exposure

The cold therapy pillar provides a ton of benefits if correctly and regularly practiced:

- Boosting immune system and sports performance
- Improving concentration and mental well-being
- Increasing willpower and energy
- Reducing inflammation, pain, and stress
- Rejuvenating skin
- Strengthening the nervous and immune system

Losing Fat

Unlike "white fat" cells that store energy derived from the food we eat, brown fat cells burn energy to release heat. Brown fat is hidden deep in the torso and neck.

Newborns are estimated to have 5 percent of brown fat in order to be able to stay warm, because they do not have the ability to shiver. After a couple of months, their brown fat significantly decreases to almost non-existent. Overheating and overdressing in our modern way of life has led almost to the disappearance of brown fat in adult bodies.

Temperatures below 19°C (66°F) generate brown fat. The lower the temperature, the more brown fat cells are created. On average, people will burn 200 calories per hour sitting in a 19° (66°) room. This is a drastic increase over the 75 calories per hour that an average person would burn.

As a conclusion, humans with higher levels of brown fat tend to have lower bodyweights and to be leaner. Let's have more brown fat cells!

My Own Result

I used to be allergic to cats. I could not approach a cat or sit on a sofa covered with cat hair without continuously sneezing. When I finished my *Wim Hof Method* training week in Poland, I could touch cats without any reactions. In less than a week of jumping into a frozen river or climbing mountains half-naked, the cold exposure changed my nervous system.

General Safety Guidelines

1. Never force any of the exercises.

2. Do not practice before consulting a medical practitioner if you have high blood pressure, cardiovascular issues, medical conditions, or are pregnant.

3. Practice in a controlled environment and with an empty stomach.

Practice

Practicing cold exposure is extremely easy, as well as time- and cost-efficient. It will become a fun experience after only three weeks of practicing. The *Reaching Impossible Limits* method incorporates four cold exercises. Gradually increase the duration of the exercises below.

Exercise 1: Room temperature. Reduce the temperature of your house to 19°C (66°F) and your bedroom to 16°C (61°F).

Exercise 2: Take cold showers. Take a daily cold shower for at least 30 seconds.

Exercise 3: Immerse your hands and feet in cold water. Put a pan filled with water in the freezer for a couple of hours. Then, immerse your hands and feet for 1 minute while watching a movie.

Exercise 4: Apply ice to your neck. Place an ice pack on the back of the neck for 20 minutes, preferably before going to bed, when insulin sensitivity is lowest.

Resources

- Online Reading

  https://onlinelibrary.wiley.com/doi/full/10.1038/oby.2010.105

- Videos

  YouTube, *Brown Fat Activation & Cold Thermogenesis*

  YouTube, *3 Methods of Cold Exposure*

Chapter 20

An Easy Process

The practice of deep in-breathing influences the ratio of oxygen (O_2) to carbon dioxide (CO_2). After a thirty-minute session of deep in-breathing, you will experience sensations of lightness, electricity, and tingling throughout your body.

> *Before climbing Mount Przesieka in Poland in extreme cold, I practiced a one-hour intense breathing session. After thirty minutes, I started experiencing unknown sensations. My body started to shake and tingle. After forty-five minutes, I went into an altered state of consciousness. I felt so much more powerful. Then I could easily climb the mountain half-naked.*

Deep In-Breathing Benefits

I recommend deep in-breathing before facing cold exposure such as taking a cold shower because of the benefits below:

- Boosting energy levels
- Decreasing stress level
- Developing better blood circulation
- Improving confidence, concentration, and focus
- Increasing VO_2 max (refer to chapter 16)

Practice

Practice 3 times a week, for 15 minutes. Refer to chapter 19 for safety guidance. (Note: It takes at least 15 minutes to feel sensations produced by the exercises.)

1. *Lie down on your back.* It is safer to lie down given the intensity of the exercise. Be comfortable and close your eyes.

2. *Take 30 power breaths.* This is essentially active, deep in-breathing at a steady pace followed by passive breaths out. Inhale fully but don't exhale all the way out. Make sure your breathing is from your belly and not from your chest. As you inhale, you should feel your belly rise, and on the exhale, you should feel your belly fall.

3. *Hold your breath.* After exhaling at 75 percent of your last 30 power breaths, hold your breath for as long as you can without forcing the hold. That's your breath retention time.

4. *Inhale and hold.* This step is optional and mostly for experienced practitioners. After your breath retention, fully inhale and hold your breath for 15 seconds.

5. *Repeat 3 times steps 2 to 4.*

6. *Do a body scan.* After completing the above exercise, you need to relax your body for at least 10 minutes. Use that time to practice the body scan technique (refer to chapter 7).

Tip: Deep in-breathing through the mouth may lead to non-controlled breathing and hyperventilation. Keep in mind that breathing through your mouth won't increase your blood oxygenation (refer to chapter 14).

Resources

- Video

  YouTube, *Wim Hof breathing tutorial by Wim Hof*

Part G

Pillar 5 – Physical Strength

Impossible Won't Exist

Chapter 21 - Use Your BMW (Bus-Metro-Walk)
The most efficient results
| 437 words | 2 minutes' reading time | 11 minutes' video time |

Chapter 22 – A Successful Lifestyle
Change your body
| 258 words | 1 minute' reading time |

Chapter 23 - Nutrition
Do not deprive
| 206 words | 1 minute' reading time |

Chapter 21

Use Your BMW (Bus-Metro-Walk)

Most of us believe we do not have enough time to exercise. The truth is that we do not have time *not to* exercise. Three hours of exercise per week is an insignificant amount of time considering the beneficial impact on the other 165 hours of the week.

An efficient exercise program includes endurance, flexibility, and strength. Its benefits to our health and body are well known:

- Enhancing muscle tone and sleep quality
- Improving our mood and brain health
- Increasing productivity and energy levels
- Promoting neuroplasticity (refer to chapter 7)

Change Your lifestyle
Before implementing a formal exercise routine, just start by moving your body whenever you get the chance.

- Take the stairs instead of elevators.
- Use your BMW (Bus-Metro-Walk) instead of driving.
- Park at least 200 meters from the store.
- Run the last 100 meters to the station to catch your train.

As stated by the 2018 US Physical Activity Guidelines Advisory Report, any movement matters for health, no matter how long it lasts.

Innovative Methods

The *Reaching Impossible Limits* method does not define a specific physical activity that you need to practice. Select one that you have fun doing, that you want to practice at least three times a week, and through which you can enhance your endurance, flexibility, and strength. The following activities are advised to train smarter, not harder.

- *Yoga.* A sequence of poses that combines relaxation techniques, controlled breathing, and stretching exercises, will speed the path to becoming a stronger, slimmer, healthier, and faster top performer. Try Kundalini yoga or Moksha yoga, which is mainly focused on the breath.

- *ChiRunning.* Sixty-five percent of all runners are estimated to incur at least one running injury a year even though the body is designed to run. The cause of these injuries is usually poor running form due to a lack of knowledge about how to run correctly.

  ChiRunning teaches people how to make running easier, more efficient, and injury-free by changing how we run. Improve your physical and mental health by practicing outside running. ChiRunning won't hurt your body.

- *Total Immersion Swimming.* Whatever your swimming experience, Total Immersion Swimming will teach you how "to cleverly adapt human anatomy to swim more like an aquatic mammal." Following a couple of easy exercises, you will become at ease in the water. Your swimming workout will evolve into a moving meditation.

Tip: Maybe you can't go the gym. In that case, download the free Nike Training app that has a huge variety of workouts. You can customize your program according to duration, equipment, activities, and intensity.

Resources
- Book

  The 4-Hour Body, Timothy Ferriss

- Online Readings

  www.chirunning.com

  www.totalimmersion.net

- Video

  YouTube, *Chi Running*

Chapter 22

A Successful Lifestyle

A healing lifestyle is as natural as breathing. It has nothing to do with seeking a miracle. Dr. Deepak Chopra says, "If we want to change the world, we have to begin by changing ourselves."

A healing lifestyle may include avoiding toxic substances like alcohol and nicotine as well as setting up your own time for a morning and evening ritual:

Morning Ritual

A morning ritual is an incredibly powerful way to start your day right. Your morning habits will lay the foundations for achieving your goals and inspiring your day. My keystone morning routine includes:

- Getting up at 6 am whatever my bedtime
- Making my bed
- Meditating for at least 30 minutes
- Practicing the power of incantations
- Taking a cold shower

When you stop thinking about and instead automatically practice new resolutions, it means you have successfully implemented a new routine. Know that it may take months of trial and error to settle on a routine. I do not make more than one change per month.

Evening Ritual

The way you end the day determines the way you start the next. Bedtime rituals can make or break your success. A night of good sleep will double the likelihood of solving a problem requiring insight.

Unplugging from electronics at least two hours before bedtime is my main evening keystone habit. Researchers have stressed that blue light emitting from electronic devices prevents your body from sleeping.

My evening ritual also includes:

- Reflecting on what happened during the day

- Reviewing my next day's schedule

- Setting my priorities for tomorrow

- Reading

Resources
- Book

  The Power of Habit, Charles Duhigg

Chapter 23

Nutrition

Scientists seem to change their minds almost every month about what kind of food is good for your body. Do not spend time reading about or following diet programs. Just eat well and simply.

How to Change Your Diet

Studies stress that almost 100 percent of people who begin dieting to lose weight fail to keep the weight off after two years. This is because diets are usually based on deprivation rather than on a gradual process of changing what one eats.

Following a slow and gradual process when changing your diet will greatly increase your odds of success. Keep your focus on one change at a time. For example, I decided to remove sugar from my daily coffee. After three weeks of slowly and daily reducing the quantity of sugar, I no longer felt the need to add it.

What to Eat and What Not to Eat

Avoid the following foods that have a negative impact on your health: processed food, refined sugar, preservatives, sodas, and alcohol. A Mediterranean diet is the preference to becoming a stronger, slimmer, healthier, and faster top performer. It incorporates the basics of healthy eating through consuming primarily plant-based foods, such as fruits and vegetables, whole grains, legumes, and nuts.

Resources

- Online Reading

  https://www.everydayhealth.com/mediterranean-diet/guide/

My Daily Program

Week 1 – My Daily Program

Exercise	Chapter	YouTube	Time	Mon	Tue	Wed	Thu	Fri	Sat	Sun
Cold shower	19		0.5 min	✓	✓	✓	✓	✓	✓	✓
BOLT score	16	How To Measure Your Control Pause?	1 min	✓	✓	✓	✓	✓	✓	✓
Changing your beliefs	4	How to Change a Belief	Tony Robbins	2 min	✓	✓		✓	✓	✓	✓
Visualize your goal	5	The Power of Visualization, The Best of Masters	2 min		✓	✓		✓	✓	
The power of incantation	6	Tony Robbins - The Power Of Incantations vs. Affirmations	2 min	✓		✓	✓		✓	✓
Meditation	7	How to Practice Vipassana Meditation in 5 Minutes	5 min	✓		✓	✓	✓		✓
Body scan	7	Body Scan Meditation - Jon Kabat-Zinn	10 min		✓		✓		✓	
Bhramari pranayama	8	Yoga Exercise To Increase Concentration - Bhramari Pranayama (Humming Bee Breath)	3 min	✓		✓		✓		✓
EFT	9	How to Tap with Jessica Ortner: Emotional Freedom Technique Informational Video	5 min	✓		✓		✓		
Breathing recovery	18	Buteyko Breathing Method - Stop Asthma Attack, Panic Attack, or Hyperventilation Attack	2 min		✓		✓		✓	
Extremity exposure	19	Complete Wim Hof Method Cold Water Routine for Feet and Hands	2 min	✓	✓		✓	✓	✓	

Week 2 – My Daily Program

Exercise	Chapter	YouTube	Time	Mon	Tue	Wed	Thu	Fri	Sat	Sun
Cold shower	19		1 min	✓	✓	✓	✓	✓	✓	✓
BOLT score	16	How To Measure Your Control Pause?	1 min	✓	✓	✓	✓	✓	✓	✓
Changing your beliefs	4	How to Change a Belief | Tony Robbins	2 min	✓		✓	✓		✓	✓
Visualize your goal	5	The Power of Visualization, The Best of Masters	2 min	✓	✓		✓	✓		✓
The power of incantation	6	Tony Robbins - The Power Of Incantations vs. Affirmations	2 min		✓	✓	✓	✓	✓	
Meditation	7	How to Practice Vipassana Meditation in 5 Minutes	5 min		✓		✓		✓	
Body scan	7	Body Scan Meditation - Jon Kabat-Zinn	15 min	✓		✓	✓	✓	✓	✓
Bhramari pranayama	8	Yoga Exercise To Increase Concentration - Bhramari Pranayama (Humming Bee Breath)	3 min	✓	✓	✓	✓	✓	✓	✓
EFT	9	How to Tap with Jessica Ortner: Emotional Freedom Technique Informational Video	5 min	✓	✓	✓	✓	✓	✓	✓
Breathing recovery	18	Buteyko Breathing Method - Stop Asthma Attack, Panic Attack, or Hyperventilation Attack	2 min	✓		✓		✓	✓	✓
Sit breathe light	18	Light Breathing Exercises - by Patrick McKeown	3 min		✓	✓	✓		✓	✓
Extremity exposure	19	Complete Wim Hof Method Cold Water Routine for Feet and Hands	2 min	✓	✓	✓	✓	✓	✓	✓

Week 3 – My Daily Program

Exercise	Chapter	YouTube	Time	Mon	Tue	Wed	Thu	Fri	Sat	Sun
Cold shower	19		1 min	✓	✓	✓	✓	✓	✓	✓
BOLT score	16	How To Measure Your Control Pause?	1 min	✓	✓	✓	✓	✓	✓	✓
Changing your beliefs	4	How to Change a Belief	Tony Robbins	3 min	✓	✓	✓	✓	✓	✓	✓
Visualize your goal	5	The Power of Visualization, The Best of Masters	3 min	✓	✓		✓	✓		✓
The power of incantation	6	Tony Robbins - The Power Of Incantations vs. Affirmations	3 min	✓	✓	✓	✓	✓	✓	✓
Meditation	7	How to Practice Vipassana Meditation in 5 Minutes	10 min	✓	✓		✓	✓	✓	
Body scan	7	Body Scan Meditation - Jon Kabat-Zinn	15 min			✓				✓
Bhramari pranayama	8	Yoga Exercise To Increase Concentration - Bhramari Pranayama (Humming Bee Breath)	5 min	✓	✓	✓	✓	✓	✓	✓
EFT	9	How to Tap with Jessica Ortner: Emotional Freedom Technique Informational Video	10 min	✓	✓	✓	✓	✓		✓
Breathing recovery	18	Buteyko Breathing Method - Stop Asthma Attack, Panic Attack, or Hyperventilation Attack	3 min		✓		✓			✓
Sit breathe light	18	Light Breathing Exercises - by Patrick McKeown	3 min	✓	✓	✓		✓	✓	
Nose unblocking	18	Unblock Your Nose Instantly by Simply Holding Your Breath	3 min	✓		✓	✓	✓	✓	
Extremity exposure	19	Complete Wim Hof Method Cold Water Routine for Feet and Hands	4 min	✓	✓	✓	✓	✓		✓

Week 4 – My Daily Program

Exercise	Chapter	YouTube	Time	Mon	Tue	Wed	Thu	Fri	Sat	Sun
Cold shower	19		2 min	✓	✓	✓	✓	✓	✓	✓
BOLT score	16	How To Measure Your Control Pause?	1 min	✓	✓	✓	✓	✓	✓	✓
Changing your beliefs	4	How to Change a Belief | Tony Robbins	4 min	✓		✓	✓		✓	✓
Visualize your goal	5	The Power of Visualization, The Best of Masters	4 min	✓	✓		✓	✓		✓
The power of incantation	6	Tony Robbins - The Power Of Incantations vs. Affirmations	4 min	✓	✓	✓		✓	✓	
Meditation	7	How to Practice Vipassana Meditation in 5 Minutes	10 min	✓	✓	✓	✓	✓		✓
Body scan	7	Body Scan Meditation - Jon Kabat-Zinn	15 min						✓	✓
Bhramari pranayama	8	Yoga Exercise To Increase Concentration - Bhramari Pranayama (Humming Bee Breath)	5 min	✓	✓	✓		✓	✓	✓
EFT	9	How to Tap with Jessica Ortner: Emotional Freedom Technique Informational Video	10 min	✓	✓	✓	✓	✓	✓	✓
Breathing recovery	18	Buteyko Breathing Method - Stop Asthma Attack, Panic Attack, or Hyperventilation Attack	3 min	✓		✓		✓		✓
Sit breathe light	18	Light Breathing Exercises - by Patrick McKeown	3 min		✓		✓		✓	
Nose unblocking	18	Unblock Your Nose Instantly by Simply Holding Your Breath	3 min	✓		✓		✓		
High altitude training	18	Simulate Altitude Training - Oxygen Advantage	5 min		✓		✓		✓	✓
Extremity exposure	19	Complete Wim Hof Method Cold Water Routine for Feet and Hands	5 min	✓		✓	✓		✓	✓

Week 5 – My Daily Customized Program

Exercise	Chapter	YouTube	Time	Mon	Tue	Wed	Thu	Fri	Sat	Sun
Cold shower	19	*How To Measure Your Control Pause?*								
BOLT score	16	*How to Change a Belief | Tony Robbins*								
Changing your beliefs	4	*The Power of Visualization, The Best of Masters*								
Visualize your goal	5	*Tony Robbins - The Power Of Incantations vs. Affirmations*								
The power of incantation	6	*How to Practice Vipassana Meditation in 5 Minutes*								
Meditation	7	*Body Scan Meditation - Jon Kabat-Zinn*								
Body scan	7	*Yoga Exercise To Increase Concentration - Bhramari Pranayama (Humming Bee Breath)*								
Bhramari pranayama	8	*How to Tap with Jessica Ortner: Emotional Freedom Technique Informational Video*								
EFT	9	*Buteyko Breathing Method - Stop Asthma Attack, Panic Attack, or Hyperventilation Attack*								
Breathing recovery	18	*Light Breathing Exercises - by Patrick McKeown*								
Sit breathe light	18	*Unblock Your Nose Instantly by Simply Holding Your Breath*								
Nose unblocking	18	*Simulate Altitude Training - Oxygen Advantage*								
High altitude training	18	*Complete Wim Hof Method Cold Water Routine for Feet and Hands*								
Extremity exposure	19									

About Reaching Impossible Limits

If you want to discuss the techniques described in this book, find research articles, provide feedback, or chat with the community, find *Reaching Impossible Limits* at our website or on the following social media platforms:

- Website

  www.reachingimpossiblelimits.com

- Facebook

  Reaching Impossible Limits

- Instagram

  @ReachingImpossibleLimits

- Twitter

  @ReachingImpossibleLimits

- YouTube

  Reaching Impossible Limits

We are stronger together; let's share our knowledge with our family, friends, community, and anyone we meet.

About Seminars and Workshops

Reaching Impossible Limits seminars and workshops are offered across the world. Check on the *Reaching Impossible Limits* website for the next events. If you have ideas for new workshop locations, let us know.